Moving Towards Sustainability: A Green Journey in Transportation

Collier Deborah Maria

Published by Collier Deborah Maria, 2024.

MOVING TOWARDS SUSTAINABILITY: A GREEN JOURNEY IN TRANSPORTATION

First edition. March 15, 2024.

Copyright © 2024 Collier Deborah Maria.

ISBN: 979-8223701873

Written by Collier Deborah Maria.

Table of Contents

Introduction. Defining Eco-friendly Transportation: Exploring the Importance of Sustainable Mobility and its Impact on Carbon Emissions 1

Chapter 1: Electric Vehicles 3

1.1 The Rise of Electric Vehicles: A Boon for Green Transportation............. 5

1.2 Benefits of Electric Vehicles: Reducing Carbon Footprint and Air Pollution 7

1.3 Challenges in Adopting Electric Vehicles: Charging Infrastructure and Cost Factors 9

1.4 Innovations and Future Prospects: Advancements in Battery Technology... 11

Chapter 2: Public Transportation 14

2.1 Role of Public Transportation in Promoting Eco-friendly Mobility..... 16

2.2 Types of Public Transportation: Buses, Trains, and Light Rail............... 18

2.3 Benefits of Public Transportation: Reducing Traffic Congestion and Air Pollution 20

2.4 Improvements Required: Enhancing Accessibility, Infrastructure, and Affordability 23

2.5 Successful Initiatives: Case Studies from Sustainable Public Transportation Systems 26

Chapter 3: Sustainable Mobility Solutions 28

3.1 Active Transportation: Walking and Cycling as Environmentally Conscious Modes.. 30

3.2 Carpooling and Ride-sharing: Reducing Emissions through Collaborative Travel 32

3.3 Advances in Green Technologies: Hydrogen Fuel Cells and Biofuels .. 34

3.4 Promoting Mixed-Use Communities: Urban Planning for Sustainable Transportation.. 37

3.5 Policy Interventions: Government Initiatives to Encourage Eco-friendly Mobility 39

Chapter 4: The Role of Urban Planning.. 42

4.1 Creating Smart Cities: Designing for Sustainable Transportation Systems 44

4.2 Integrating Land-use and Transportation: Efficient City Development 46

4.3 Public Spaces and Pedestrian-friendly Infrastructure: Encouraging Active Transportation 48

4.4 Prioritizing Public Transportation: Transit-oriented Development and Walkability Strategies 50

4.5 Strengthening Non-motorized Transportation Networks: Safe and Connected Cycling and Walking Paths 52

Chapter 5: Global Trends in Eco-friendly Transportation 55

5.1 Comparative Analysis: Eco-friendly Transportation Initiatives around the World 57

5.2 Success Stories: Cities and Countries Leading the Charge towards Sustainability 59

5.3 Challenges and Opportunities: Adapting Best Practices in Different Regions 61

5.4 International Collaboration: Global Efforts towards Climate-Resilient Transportation Systems 63

Conclusion. Addressing Climate Change through Eco-friendly Transportation: Taking Steps towards a Greener Future 65

Introduction. Defining Eco-friendly Transportation: Exploring the Importance of Sustainable Mobility and its Impact on Carbon Emissions

Transportation plays a crucial role in our daily lives as it provides us with the means to explore our surroundings, commute to work, and visit loved ones. However, with the rise in carbon emissions and the negative impact on the environment, there has been a growing need for eco-friendly transportation options. In this essay, we will define eco-friendly transportation, explore its importance in sustainable mobility, and understand its significant impact on reducing carbon emissions.

The term "eco-friendly transportation" refers to the use of vehicles and modes of transport that have minimal negative impact on the environment. This encompasses a wide range of vehicles and technologies designed to minimize carbon emissions, reduce fuel consumption, and promote sustainable practices. It includes not only electric vehicles but also bicycles, public transportation systems, and other alternatives to private cars that contribute to a greener society.

One of the most significant advantages of eco-friendly transportation is its ability to promote sustainable mobility. Sustainable mobility emphasizes the efficient and convenient movement of people and goods while minimizing negative environmental and societal impacts. It involves the integration of different transportation modes, encouraging the use of public transportation, cycling paths, and walkable communities. By providing a variety of choices for individuals, sustainable mobility aims to reduce traffic congestion, air pollution, and dependence on fossil fuels.

The importance of sustainable mobility cannot be overstated. As the global population continues to grow, cities become more crowded, and pollution levels rise, finding ways to reduce carbon emissions becomes increasingly urgent. Eco-friendly transportation options, such as electric vehicles and cycling infrastructure, offer sustainable solutions to these pressing challenges. By reducing the reliance on fossil fuels, sustainable mobility can help mitigate air pollution, improve public health, and combat global climate change.

Moreover, the impact of eco-friendly transportation on carbon emissions cannot be ignored. According to the Intergovernmental Panel on Climate Change (IPCC), the transportation sector accounts for approximately one-quarter of global carbon dioxide (CO_2) emissions, making it a significant contributor to climate change. By transitioning to eco-friendly transportation options, we can significantly reduce these emissions. Electric vehicles, for instance, produce zero tailpipe emissions, making them an essential part of the solution. When coupled with efforts to decarbonize the electricity generation sector, electric vehicles can be a game-changer in curbing carbon emissions from transportation.

In conclusion, eco-friendly transportation offers a sustainable and environmentally friendly alternative to traditional modes of transportation. By promoting sustainable mobility and reducing carbon emissions, it addresses the pressing challenges of air pollution, climate change, and the need for a greener future. Advancements in technology, public policy, and individual choices are vital in supporting the transition to eco-friendly transportation, ultimately leading to a greener and more sustainable world.

Chapter 1: Electric Vehicles

Electric vehicles (EVs) have taken the world by storm in recent years, emerging as a crucial player in the field of green transportation. The quest for sustainable and eco-friendly alternatives to traditional internal combustion engine vehicles has led to the remarkable rise of EVs, setting a new benchmark for the automotive industry.

The mindset behind the creation of electric vehicles is simple yet revolutionary—to provide efficient and sustainable transportation that drastically lowers greenhouse gas emissions. With the steady decline in fossil fuel reserves and the urgent need to mitigate climate change, the shift towards EVs has become imperative. This transition has not only opened up a host of opportunities but also created a paradigm shift in the perception of automotive transportation.

EVs are powered primarily by electricity stored in battery packs, which can be charged using electric power stations. The battery technology has evolved significantly over the years, from the early days of nickel-metal hydride batteries to the more advanced lithium-ion batteries that now dominate the market. These lithium-ion batteries offer higher energy density, longer driving ranges, and faster charging times, making them the preferred choice for many automakers.

One of the biggest advantages of electric vehicles is their minimal or zero tailpipe emissions. Unlike gasoline or diesel-fueled vehicles, which emit harmful pollutants such as carbon dioxide, nitrogen oxides, and particulate matter, EVs produce no exhaust emissions. This not only contributes to improved air quality but also helps in combating the growing problem of pollution-related health issues.

Moreover, electric vehicles play a significant role in reducing our carbon footprint. By using electricity from renewable sources like solar or wind, EVs effectively eliminate the greenhouse gas emissions associated with electricity generation. This makes them an important tool in tackling the global climate crisis.

The rise of EVs has also led to technological advancements and innovation in the automotive industry. Automakers are investing heavily in research and development to improve battery technology, increase driving ranges, and create more efficient electric drivetrains. These innovations have led to substantial improvement in the performance of electric cars, with some models now posing serious competition to their combustion engine counterparts in terms of acceleration and top speed.

Furthermore, the decreasing cost of lithium-ion batteries, spurred by advancements in manufacturing processes and economies of scale, has made EVs more attainable for a larger consumer base. The initial high purchase cost of electric vehicles has been a thorny issue for many potential buyers, but as the technology matures and becomes more widespread, costs are coming down, making EVs a viable option for more consumers worldwide.

The benefits of electric vehicles extend beyond their environmental impact. The electric drivetrain offers a smooth and silent driving experience, reducing noise pollution in urban areas. This is particularly advantageous for densely populated cities, where noise pollution can have detrimental effects on human health and wellbeing.

In conclusion, the rise of electric vehicles has brought about significant transformations in the automotive industry and the broader field of green transportation. These vehicles offer an eco-friendly alternative to conventional gasoline or diesel-fueled vehicles, reducing greenhouse gas emissions and promoting a sustainable future. With advancements in battery technology, decreasing costs, and increased consumer interest, electric vehicles are poised to play a crucial role in shaping the transportation landscape of the future.

1.1 The Rise of Electric Vehicles: A Boon for Green Transportation

Electric vehicles (EVs) have gained tremendous popularity in recent years, and for good reason. One of the most significant benefits of EVs is their ability to reduce the carbon footprint and combat air pollution. Let's dive deeper into these benefits to understand their impact on the environment.

Reducing greenhouse gas emissions is crucial in the fight against climate change, and EVs play a pivotal role in achieving this goal. Unlike conventional gasoline-powered vehicles, EVs run on electricity, which can be sourced from renewable energy sources such as solar or wind power. This drastically reduces the amount of greenhouse gases emitted during the vehicle's operation.

The transportation sector is a significant contributor to greenhouse gas emissions, particularly carbon dioxide (CO_2). According to the International Energy Agency, it accounted for about 24% of global CO_2 emissions from fuel combustion in 2019. By transitioning to EVs, we can reduce these emissions and mitigate the detrimental effects of climate change. Estimates suggest that EVs produce about 50-60% fewer CO_2 emissions compared to conventional vehicles throughout their lifetime.

Another pollutant emitted by traditional vehicles is nitrogen oxide (NOx), which contributes to air pollution and poses serious health risks. NOx is a major contributor to the formation of smog and can cause respiratory problems. EVs have zero tailpipe emissions, meaning they do not emit any NOx directly. Even when accounting for the emissions from electricity generation, which might come from power plants burning fossil fuels, EVs are still generally cleaner and emit fewer harmful pollutants than conventional vehicles.

In addition to reducing greenhouse gas emissions and air pollution, EVs offer the potential to improve local air quality. Many cities struggle with air pollution, particularly in densely populated areas with heavy traffic. Combustion engine vehicles release particulate matter and other harmful pollutants into the air, leading to increased respiratory issues and decreased overall well-being. EVs can help alleviate this problem by producing zero tailpipe emissions, thus eliminating one major source of air pollution.

Moreover, the adoption of EVs promotes the use of renewable energy, such as solar and wind power. As more EVs hit the road, the demand for electricity will increase, spurring the need to invest in renewable energy infrastructure. This acceleration of clean energy adoption creates a positive feedback loop, as more renewable energy generation will lead to even lower greenhouse gas emissions.

In conclusion, the benefits of electric vehicles when it comes to reducing carbon footprint and air pollution cannot be understated. By transitioning from traditional vehicles to EVs, we can significantly decrease greenhouse gas emissions, combat air pollution, and improve local air quality. Furthermore, the widespread adoption of EVs can accelerate the shift towards renewable energy sources and ultimately contribute to a more sustainable and greener future.

1.2 Benefits of Electric Vehicles: Reducing Carbon Footprint and Air Pollution

The transition to electric vehicles (EVs) is seen as a crucial step in reducing the carbon footprint of transportation and moving towards a sustainable future. However, adopting electric vehicles does come with its fair share of challenges. Two main challenges that hinder the widespread adoption of EVs are charging infrastructure and cost factors.

1. Charging Infrastructure:

One of the major obstacles in the adoption of electric vehicles is the lack of an extensive and reliable charging infrastructure. Unlike conventional gasoline vehicles that can be refueled at gas stations readily available all over the country, EVs require charging stations to recharge their batteries.

However, in many areas, especially in rural and suburban regions, there is a scarcity of charging stations. This limitation prompts "range anxiety" among potential EV buyers, fearing that they may run out of battery power during their journeys and not be able to find a charging point. This lack of charging infrastructure discourages people from considering EVs as a viable option, even if they are environmentally conscious.

Furthermore, the existing charging infrastructure also faces challenges concerning the speed of charging. Fast-charging stations that can rapidly replenish an EV's battery are more limited in number compared to slower chargers, adding to the inconvenience for EV owners.

Although efforts are being made to expand the charging infrastructure, including public-private partnerships and increased government investment, progress has been slow. Overcoming this challenge requires a significant investment in charging infrastructure, along with a well-thought-out plan for its deployment and expansion across cities, suburbs, and rural areas.

2. Cost Factors:

Another significant obstacle in the mass adoption of electric vehicles is the initial purchasing cost. EVs, particularly models with extended driving ranges or high-performance capabilities, tend to be more expensive than their gasoline-powered counterparts. This higher cost stems from the expenses associated with developing electric propulsion systems, advanced lithium-ion batteries, and other unique components utilized in EVs.

Although operational costs for EVs are typically lower due to lower electricity prices when compared to gasoline prices, the higher upfront cost can deter potential buyers. Many consumers are unwilling to invest in electric vehicles due to the initial cost exceeding their budget or the perceived lack of return on investment.

Moreover, electric vehicle buyers may also face challenges related to battery replacement costs. Even though EV batteries are designed to last for several years, replacing a faulty or worn-out battery can incur significant expenses. This cost factor raises concerns about the overall lifetime expenses of electric vehicles.

To overcome the cost challenge, various measures are being implemented. These include government rebates and incentives, which reduce the purchase price of electric vehicles and make them more affordable for consumers. Additionally, advancements in battery technology and manufacturing processes are leading to reductions in production costs, which can eventually translate into more cost-effective electric vehicles.

In conclusion, while the transition to electric vehicles is essential for a more sustainable future, it is crucial to address the challenges hindering their widespread adoption. The limited charging infrastructure and higher upfront costs are significant obstacles that can discourage potential buyers. By investing in charging infrastructure expansion and offering incentives to mitigate the cost challenges, we can facilitate the wider adoption of electric vehicles and steer towards a greener transportation sector.

1.3 Challenges in Adopting Electric Vehicles: Charging Infrastructure and Cost Factors

1.4 Innovations and Future Prospects: Advancements in Battery Technology

• • • •

BATTERY TECHNOLOGY has come a long way since its inception, powering everything from our everyday gadgets to electric vehicles. With the increasing demand for energy storage solutions and renewable energy sources, innovations in battery technology have become vital. In this section, we will delve into the latest advancements and future prospects in battery technology.

1. Solid-State Batteries:

One of the most exciting breakthroughs in battery technology is the development of solid-state batteries. Unlike traditional lithium-ion batteries, which use liquid electrolytes, solid-state batteries employ solid electrolytes. This eliminates the risk of leakage, enhances the overall safety, and increases the energy density of the battery. Solid-state batteries have the potential to revolutionize the electric vehicle industry, providing longer ranges and faster charging times.

2. Lithium-Sulfur Batteries:

Lithium-sulfur batteries are another next-generation technology on the horizon. They offer higher energy densities, potentially up to five times greater than current lithium-ion batteries. By utilizing sulfur as the cathode material instead of the conventional graphite, lithium-sulfur batteries can offer lighter, more compact energy storage solutions with extended range capabilities. Although challenges like the short lifespan of the battery still need to be addressed, lithium-sulfur batteries hold immense potential for both portable electronics and electric vehicles.

3. Flow Batteries:

Flow batteries are a promising energy storage technology that utilizes two tanks of electrolyte solutions to store and release energy. Unlike traditional batteries, flow batteries offer scalability and flexibility as they separate the storage capacity from the power output. This makes them highly suitable for grid-level applications where storing excess energy generated by renewable sources is crucial. Flow batteries have a longer cycle life and retain their capacity over time, which makes them an attractive prospect for large-scale energy storage and integration with renewable energy systems.

4. Advanced materials and manufacturing techniques:

Recent developments in material science and manufacturing techniques have also contributed to advancements in battery technology. Researchers are exploring new materials such as silicon, the anode's primary component, to improve energy densities and cycling capabilities further. Moreover, advanced manufacturing techniques like 3D printing enable the production of complex battery designs, allowing for optimized energy storage based on specific applications. Such advancements in materials and manufacturing processes are propelling battery technology towards greater efficiency and performance.

5. Recycling and environmental concerns:

With the increasing adoption of rechargeable batteries, proper management of battery waste has become crucial. Innovations in battery technology must go hand in hand with sustainable practices and recycling initiatives. Researchers are developing efficient methods to recover valuable materials, including lithium, cobalt, and nickel, from discarded batteries to lessen the environmental impact and minimize the reliance on scarce resources. Developing closed-loop recycling systems will be critical for sustainable battery technology in the future.

• • • •

ADVANCEMENTS IN BATTERY technology hold immense promise for a greener and more sustainable future. Solid-state batteries, lithium-sulfur batteries, and flow batteries are among the most notable innovations that could revolutionize energy storage in various industries. Moreover, the continuous development of advanced materials and manufacturing techniques, coupled with recycling initiatives, will ensure the long-term viability of battery technology. As research and investment in this field continue to grow, we can expect significant improvements in energy storage, longer-lasting batteries, and increased renewable energy integration into the global power grid.

1.4 Innovations and Future Prospects: Advancements in Battery Technology

Chapter 2: Public Transportation

Public transportation plays a crucial role in the lives of millions of people worldwide. It enables individuals to move efficiently and affordably, connecting them to various destinations within their communities and beyond. This chapter will explore the intricacies of public transportation and delve into the various modes available, their benefits, and challenges.

Public transportation encompasses different modes such as buses, trains, trams, subways, and ferries. Each mode serves specific purposes, catering to the diverse needs of commuters. Buses, for instance, are the most widely used mode of public transportation, offering extensive coverage across urban, suburban, and rural areas. Their flexibility, affordability, and convenience make them a preferred choice for many passengers. Trains, on the other hand, are ideal for long-distance travel, allowing commuters to cover considerable distances comfortably and swiftly. These trains are often equipped with amenities like restaurants, sleeping compartments, and entertainment options, providing an enhanced travel experience.

Moreover, trams and subways offer fast and efficient transportation within cities, mitigating traffic congestion and reducing emissions. Trams generally operate on dedicated tracks running along city streets, blending seamlessly with the urban landscape, while subways run underground, ensuring an uninterrupted commute through crowded areas. These modes attract individuals due to their speed, reliability, and capacity to transport large volumes of passengers efficiently.

Additionally, ferry services play a crucial role in cities bordering water bodies or coastal areas by connecting various points and facilitating both passenger and cargo movement. They serve as crucial links for residents of coastal neighborhoods, providing an alternative mode of transportation and reducing dependence on road networks.

Public transportation offers countless benefits, impacting not only individuals but also society and the environment. One of the key advantages is the reduction of traffic congestion. The use of public transportation enables the consolidation of commuters, significantly reducing the number of individual vehicles on the road. As a result, traffic congestion decreases, leading to shorter travel times and a more efficient transportation system. This congestion alleviation benefits not only those who use public transportation but also private vehicle users, who experience reduced delays and improved overall travel experience.

Public transportation also contributes to environmental sustainability. With a higher number of individuals opting for public transport, the overall carbon footprint decreases. Public transportation systems, especially electric buses and trains, contribute to reducing greenhouse gas emissions and air pollution, making cities cleaner and healthier places to live. Additionally, fewer vehicles on the road result in reduced noise pollution, leading to improved quality of life for people residing near busy thoroughfares.

Furthermore, public transportation provides increased accessibility and mobility for those who may not own private vehicles. It ensures equitable access to essential services, employment opportunities, education, and healthcare. Public transportation connects individuals and communities, bridging geographical divides and promoting social cohesion. It enables individuals of all income levels to travel affordably, eliminating economic barriers and fostering inclusivity within society.

However, public transportation also faces various challenges. One common issue is funding. The development, maintenance, and operation of public transportation systems require substantial investments from government agencies. Insufficient funds may lead to inadequate coverage, outdated infrastructure, and decreased service quality. Public transportation agencies need sustainable funding models to ensure reliable services and continuous improvements.

Another challenge lies in providing frequent and reliable service. Passengers' trust in public transportation is directly related to its punctuality and consistency. Delays, long waiting times, and erratic schedules can deter people from opting for these modes. Therefore, transportation authorities must prioritize timely schedules and effective communication to cater to passenger needs and attract more users.

Moreover, addressing safety concerns is vital to maintain public trust. Passengers should feel secure while using public transportation systems. The authorities must implement robust safety measures, including security personnel, surveillance, and emergency protocols, to create a comfortable, secure atmosphere for all commuters. Regular maintenance and inspections of vehicles and infrastructure are also essential to avoid accidents and ensure passenger safety.

In conclusion, public transportation constitutes an integral component of urban and rural mobility. Various modes such as buses, trains, trams, subways, and ferries cater to an array of transportation needs, offering numerous benefits. Public transportation decreases traffic congestion, reduces environmental impact, enhances accessibility and mobility, and fosters social inclusion. Nonetheless, challenges regarding funding, service quality, and safety must be addressed to ensure the effectiveness and popularity of public transportation systems. By investing in reliable infrastructure, ensuring appropriate funding, and prioritizing passengers' needs, public transportation can continue to play a pivotal role in shaping sustainable, connected, and accessible communities.

Chapter 2: Public Transportation

Public transportation plays a crucial role in promoting eco-friendly mobility. As cities continue to grow and urbanization becomes a global trend, the need for efficient and sustainable transportation options becomes increasingly important. Public transportation not only provides a viable alternative to individual car ownership but also contributes to reducing air pollution, conserving energy, and improving the overall quality of life in cities.

One of the primary ways public transportation promotes eco-friendly mobility is by reducing the number of cars on the road. Private vehicles are a significant source of greenhouse gas emissions and air pollution. By offering convenient, reliable, and affordable alternatives, such as buses, trains, trams, and subways, public transportation encourages people to ditch their cars and opt for a more sustainable mode of transport. This, in turn, helps reduce congestion and emissions, leading to improved air quality and a healthier environment for everyone.

Moreover, public transportation serves as a key component in creating more sustainable and compact cities. By providing efficient transportation networks that connect various urban areas, it enables better land use patterns that can maximize density and minimize sprawl. This ultimately reduces the need for long-distance commuting, which can result in lower energy consumption, less traffic congestion, and, consequently, lower emissions.

Public transportation also contributes to decreasing energy consumption and dependence on fossil fuels. Compared to individual cars, public transportation vehicles consume significantly less energy to transport a larger number of passengers per trip. Additionally, the adoption of eco-friendly technologies, such as electric or hybrid buses and trains, further reduces carbon emissions and reliance on non-renewable energy sources. By prioritizing sustainable practices and investing in cleaner technologies, public transportation authorities become pioneers in promoting eco-friendly mobility.

Beyond the environmental benefits, public transportation also enhances social and economic equality within a city. It provides a more accessible and affordable mode of transport for people from diverse socio-economic backgrounds, reducing the transportation burden for low-income communities that may face challenges in owning a private vehicle. Sustainable mobility options also contribute to improved social cohesion by fostering inclusive communities where people of all ages, abilities, and backgrounds can easily access essential services, education, and employment opportunities.

In recent years, the importance of public transportation in combatting climate change and achieving sustainable development goals has gained increasing recognition from governments, policymakers, and urban planners. Many cities have made considerable investments to expand and improve their public transportation networks, introducing innovative approaches and technologies to support eco-friendly mobility. These initiatives include the integration of smart transportation systems, the development of cycling and pedestrian-friendly infrastructure, and the introduction of shared mobility solutions like carpooling and bike-sharing schemes.

In conclusion, the role of public transportation in promoting eco-friendly mobility cannot be overstated. Through reducing car usage, encouraging sustainable urban development, decreasing energy consumption, and fostering social equality, public transportation plays a pivotal role in building greener and more livable cities. Governments and policymakers should prioritize investing in and expanding public transportation options to create a sustainable future for all.

2.1 Role of Public Transportation in Promoting Eco-friendly Mobility

Public transportation plays a crucial role in promoting eco-friendly mobility and sustainable transportation systems. It serves as a viable alternative to private vehicle usage, reducing traffic congestion, energy consumption, and greenhouse gas emissions. In this article, we will delve into the specific impact that public transportation has on promoting environmentally friendly mobility.

Firstly, public transportation helps to mitigate traffic congestion by providing an efficient means of transportation for a large number of people. By encouraging people to utilize public transportation services, it reduces the number of private vehicles on the road, which contributes to streamlined traffic flow. This not only enhances travel time for commuters but also leads to a reduction in fuel consumption and air pollution caused by idle vehicles in congested areas.

Secondly, public transportation is an integral part of a sustainable and integrated transportation system. It provides connectivity between different modes of transport such as metros, buses, trams, and trains. The integration of various transportation options enables individuals to choose the most appropriate and convenient mode of travel for their needs. This user-centric approach reduces unnecessary travel distances, promotes intermodal connectivity, and eliminates the need for private vehicles for every trip, leading to a significant reduction in carbon emissions.

Furthermore, public transportation plays a crucial role in reducing energy consumption associated with mobility. Public transit systems are designed to be more energy-efficient compared to private vehicles. They utilize engines with higher fuel efficiency and are optimized to carry large numbers of passengers, thus reducing the overall energy consumption per person. Apart from the direct impact on energy consumption, public transportation infrastructure, particularly electrically powered systems such as electric buses or trains, can contribute to the decarbonization of the transport sector by utilizing clean and renewable energy sources.

Public transportation networks can also facilitate environmentally friendly commuting alternatives, such as cycling or walking. By providing infrastructure such as bike racks, pedestrian paths, and bike-sharing facilities, public transit systems can encourage individuals to combine cycling or walking with their public transit journey. This integrated approach promotes sustainable modes of transportation, reduces dependency on private vehicles, and leads to healthier lifestyles.

Additionally, public transportation has beneficial economic impacts that contribute to the promotion of eco-friendly mobility. Reliable and accessible public transportation can improve the overall efficiency of a city by reducing time wasted in traffic and increasing productivity. This strategic investment enhances accessibility to employment opportunities, educational institutions, and other essential services, supporting economic development and reducing socio-economic inequalities. By creating job opportunities in the public transportation sector, the development of eco-friendly mobility options can also contribute to regional economic growth.

In conclusion, public transportation plays a significant role in promoting eco-friendly mobility and sustainable transportation systems. Through the reduction of traffic congestion, energy consumption, and greenhouse gas emissions, public transit systems offer a viable alternative to private vehicles while providing efficient and interconnected transportation services. Additionally, public transportation networks can facilitate the integration of cycling and walking, contributing to healthier and sustainable lifestyles. The economic benefits of public transportation further consolidate its role in promoting environmentally friendly mobility. Thus, supporting and prioritizing public transportation projects and initiatives should be a key focus to achieve a greener and more sustainable future.

2.2 Types of Public Transportation: Buses, Trains, and Light Rail

Public transportation has numerous benefits, and two of them are especially significant: reducing traffic congestion and air pollution. In today's world, where road congestion and environmental pollution are major concerns, public transportation emerges as a viable solution.

First and foremost, public transportation plays an essential role in alleviating traffic congestion. In cities and urban areas, traffic congestion has become a major problem. With the increase in population and vehicles on the road, more and more people find themselves stuck in traffic jams on a daily basis. This not only wastes valuable time but also increases stress and frustration levels. Public transportation systems, such as buses and trains, provide an alternative to private cars, reducing the number of vehicles on the road and subsequently decreasing traffic congestion. By encouraging people to leave their cars at home and use public transportation, cities can experience smoother traffic flow, shorter commute times, and less gridlock.

Furthermore, public transportation has a significant impact on reducing air pollution. The transportation sector is a major contributor to air pollution, releasing harmful pollutants into the atmosphere. Private cars emit greenhouse gases, including carbon dioxide and nitrogen oxides, which contribute to global warming and air pollution. On the other hand, public transportation vehicles tend to be more fuel-efficient and emit fewer pollutants per passenger. By promoting the use of public transportation, cities can lower their carbon footprint and improve air quality. This has direct health benefits, as air pollution is a leading cause of respiratory diseases and other health conditions.

Investing in public transportation also has long-term economic advantages. Traffic congestion slows down economic activity, leading to productivity losses and increased fuel consumption. By reducing traffic congestion, public transportation helps facilitate the movement of people and goods, supporting economic growth and efficiency. Furthermore, it can save individuals money, as the cost of using public transportation is often cheaper than maintaining a private vehicle. This is particularly beneficial for low-income individuals who may struggle to afford car ownership.

MOVING TOWARDS SUSTAINABILITY: A GREEN JOURNEY IN TRANSPORTATION

In addition, public transportation promotes social equity by providing equal access to transportation options for all members of society. It ensures that people who cannot afford or are unable to drive have a reliable means of transport. By reducing reliance on cars, public transportation enhances mobility and inclusivity, leading to a more connected and cohesive community.

In conclusion, public transportation offers several benefits, including reducing traffic congestion and air pollution. By providing an alternative to private cars, public transportation decreases the number of vehicles on the road, resulting in reduced traffic congestion and quicker commute times. Moreover, it improves air quality by emitting fewer pollutants per passenger compared to individual vehicles. Additionally, investing in public transportation has economic advantages, supports social equity, and contributes to a greener and more sustainable future. Promoting and expanding public transportation systems should be a priority for governments and policymakers worldwide, as they bring about numerous societal and environmental benefits.

2.3 Benefits of Public Transportation: Reducing Traffic Congestion and Air Pollution

In order to improve accessibility, infrastructure, and affordability, several improvements are required. These improvements are essential to ensure that individuals have equal opportunities to access and benefit from various services and resources within a society. Here, we will focus on important areas where enhancements are necessary.

1. Enhancing Accessibility:

Accessibility refers to the ease and convenience of accessing certain facilities, services, and opportunities without any physical or social barriers. It is crucial to create an inclusive environment where individuals with disabilities, elderly individuals, and those with limited mobility can participate fully in society. To enhance accessibility, the following measures can be taken:

a) Constructing Ramp and Widening Doors: Public buildings, transportation systems, and other vital infrastructure need to have ramps and wider doors to cater to individuals who use wheelchairs or other mobility aids. This will provide them with a barrier-free access experience.

b) Installing Elevators and Lifts: Elevators and lifts should be installed in multi-story buildings, transportation stations, and other public spaces. This will enable people with mobility challenges to easily move between different floors and access various facilities.

c) Implementing Sensory Enhancements: For individuals with visual or hearing impairments, it is crucial to provide sensory enhancements. This includes installing tactile signs, providing audio announcements in public transportation systems, and employing guiding devices like Braille signage.

d) Promoting Digital Accessibility: With the advent of digital technologies, it is important to ensure that online platforms and services are accessible for individuals with disabilities. Websites and applications should conform to accessibility standards, offering assistive technologies like screen readers and keyboard navigation.

2. Improving Infrastructure:

MOVING TOWARDS SUSTAINABILITY: A GREEN JOURNEY IN TRANSPORTATION

Infrastructure development plays a key role in enhancing the overall quality of life and economic growth. To ensure improvements in this aspect, the following steps can be taken:

a) Upgrading Transportation Systems: Equitable access to transportation is vital for individuals to reach job opportunities, educational institutions, healthcare services, and social events. Investments should be made in expanding public transportation networks, improving connectivity between rural and urban areas, and ensuring affordability.

b) Strengthening Communication Networks: Access to high-speed, reliable internet and mobile phone connectivity is essential to bridge the digital divide. Governments should invest in expanding broadband infrastructure in underserved areas and lowering internet costs to enable equal access for all.

c) Renewable Energy Provision: Transitioning towards sustainable and renewable energy sources is imperative. Governments should invest in developing renewable energy infrastructure, such as solar and wind power, for cleaner and affordable energy options that benefit all citizens.

d) Upgrading Water and Sanitation Systems: Access to clean water and improved sanitation facilities is a basic human right. Governments should invest in improving water supply systems, wastewater treatment plants, and sanitation facilities in underserved areas, ensuring better health and well-being for all.

3. Ensuring Affordability:

Affordability is crucial in enabling individuals to access essential goods and services, ensuring their overall well-being. To improve affordability, the following steps can be taken:

a) Affordable Housing Initiatives: Governments can introduce policies that promote affordable housing by offering subsidies, tax incentives, or partnering with private entities to increase the supply of affordable housing units. This will help mitigate the issue of rising housing costs and ensure stable, affordable shelter for all.

b) Accessible Healthcare Services: Healthcare should be affordable and easily accessible to all individuals. Governments can implement measures like public health insurance schemes, subsidized healthcare facilities, and ensuring the provision of quality healthcare in remote and underserved areas.

c) Education Reforms: Access to quality education is vital for personal growth and socio-economic mobility. Governments should invest in educational infrastructure, offer scholarships, and incentivize public-private partnerships to make education more affordable and accessible.

d) Price Regulation: Authorities should monitor and regulate prices of essential goods and services to protect consumers from exorbitant costs. This can range from regulating pharmaceutical prices to ensuring fair pricing in utilities like electricity, water, and gas.

By implementing these improvements, society can become more inclusive, enabling individuals from all walks of life to access and benefit from various resources and opportunities. Enhancing accessibility, infrastructure, and affordability should be of utmost importance to governments, organizations, and individuals alike, as it ultimately leads to a more equitable and prosperous society for all.

2.4 Improvements Required: Enhancing Accessibility, Infrastructure, and Affordability

2.5 Successful Initiatives: Case Studies from Sustainable Public Transportation Systems

· · · ·

AS CITIES ACROSS THE globe grapple with issues such as traffic congestion, pollution, and limited resources, the development of sustainable transportation systems has become a pressing issue. In this article, we present in-depth case studies of 2.5 successful initiatives that have transformed public transportation systems into sustainable alternatives. The aim is to analyze the elements that contribute to their success and the lessons they offer for future initiatives.

1. The Curitiba Bus Rapid Transit System, Brazil:

The city of Curitiba in Brazil has long been hailed as a model for sustainable public transportation. The introduction of a Bus Rapid Transit (BRT) system in the city was a visionary move that revolutionized the way people commute. The key features of this initiative are:

- Dedicated bus lanes: Curitiba implemented a system of dedicated bus lanes which reduced travel times, decreased pollution levels, and minimized traffic congestion.

- Integration with urban planning: The BRT system in Curitiba was seamlessly integrated with the city's urban planning. This allowed for efficient connectivity with other modes of transport, including cycling and walking.

- Incentivizing ridership: Curitiba implemented various measures to attract more people to use public transportation, such as low fares, user-friendly stations, and comfortable buses. The result was a significant increase in ridership.

2. Tokyo's Rail Transit System, Japan:

Tokyo's rail transit system exemplifies Japan's commitment to sustainable transportation. The city's rail networks are known for their punctuality, reliability, and remarkable efficiency. Key factors that contribute to its success include:

- Comprehensive coverage: Tokyo's rail system covers a vast network, connecting even the most remote parts of the city. This extensive coverage encourages people to rely on public transportation instead of private cars.

- Integration of technologies: Tokyo's rail system effectively integrates advanced technologies such as electronic ticketing systems, real-time information displays, and energy-efficient trains. These innovations enhance the overall efficiency and experience for commuters.

- Public-private partnerships: Tokyo's rail system leverage collaborations with various stakeholders, including private companies, for smooth operations and infrastructure maintenance. This partnership helps optimize resources and reduce operational costs.

3. Cycling Infrastructure in Copenhagen, Denmark:

Copenhagen has garnered global attention for promoting cycling as a sustainable alternative to traditional transportation methods. Notable elements of this successful initiative include:

- Safe infrastructure: Copenhagen's cycling infrastructure emphasizes well-designed bike lanes, separate signals, and storage facilities. This ensures the safety and convenience of cyclists, encouraging more people to embrace cycling as a viable mode of transportation.

- Cultural transformation: The initiative addressed the cultural barriers associated with cycling by promoting a positive image of cycling and a societal shift towards embracing it. Public awareness campaigns, cycling education, and events played significant roles in this transformation.

- Urban planning integration: Copenhagen's cycling infrastructure is seamlessly integrated into the overall city planning process. This collaboration between transportation planners and urban designers enables the incorporation of cycling as a fundamental element of urban development.

• • • •

THROUGH THESE CASE studies, we witness how creative and visionary approaches to sustainable public transportation can transform cities. The success stories of the Curitiba BRT system, Tokyo's rail transit, and Copenhagen's cycling infrastructure demonstrate that sustainable transportation is achievable through dedicated planning, integration, partnerships, and cultural transformation. The lessons learned from these initiatives serve as inspiration and guidelines for future sustainable transportation endeavors around the world.

25

2.5 Successful Initiatives: Case Studies from Sustainable Public Transportation Systems

Chapter 3: Sustainable Mobility Solutions

As the world becomes more urbanized and connected, finding sustainable mobility solutions has become vital to ensuring a livable and resilient future. The need to reduce greenhouse gas emissions, alleviate traffic congestion, and improve air quality has led to the development of various innovative ideas and technologies. In this chapter, we will explore some of these promising solutions that aim to revolutionize transportation systems and make them more sustainable.

One exciting development in sustainable mobility is the rise of electric vehicles (EVs). Powered by rechargeable lithium-ion batteries, EVs produce zero tailpipe emissions, reducing air pollution and dependence on fossil fuels. Many countries and cities have set ambitious targets to phase out internal combustion engine vehicles and promote electric mobility. Moreover, advancements in battery technology have increased the range and efficiency of EVs, making them more practical for everyday use.

However, the widespread adoption of EVs also presents challenges. Limited charging infrastructure, high costs, and concerns about battery life and range anxiety remain roadblocks to their mass-market adoption. To address these issues, innovative solutions are being implemented. For instance, fast-charging stations are being installed along highways and in urban areas to improve charging infrastructure. Additionally, research is underway to develop more affordable and efficient batteries with extended range.

Another sustainable mobility solution gaining traction is the concept of shared mobility. Instead of individual car ownership, shared mobility services promote the utilization of vehicles on a pay-per-use basis. This reduces the overall number of vehicles on the road and makes transportation more efficient and cost-effective. Ridesharing platforms like Uber and Lyft have revolutionized urban transportation, encouraging people to forego car ownership in favor of shared rides.

Furthermore, bike-sharing and scooter-sharing programs have become popular in cities around the world. These systems provide access to bicycles and

MOVING TOWARDS SUSTAINABILITY: A GREEN JOURNEY IN TRANSPORTATION

electric scooters for short trips within urban areas, reducing the reliance on cars for short-distance travel. Additionally, integrating bike lanes and improving pedestrian infrastructure has encouraged active modes of transportation, promoting healthier and emission-free mobility options.

Innovative technologies like autonomous vehicles (AVs) also hold promise for sustainable mobility. AVs have the potential to significantly reduce traffic congestion and improve road safety by eliminating human error. Moreover, coordinated routing and platooning techniques can enhance the efficiency of AVs, reducing energy consumption and carbon emissions. However, key challenges such as regulatory frameworks, liability issues, and public acceptance need to be addressed before AVs can become mainstream.

Furthermore, sustainable mobility solutions go beyond just electrification and shared mobility. Smart transportation systems that optimize traffic flow, reduce congestion, and minimize delays are being developed. Intelligent transportation management systems use real-time data and advanced analytics to prioritize and regulate traffic, improving overall efficiency. Moreover, integrating various modes of transportation, such as buses, trains, and cycling, into a seamless multimodal network can further enhance mobility options.

In conclusion, sustainable mobility solutions are essential for tackling the environmental and societal challenges posed by urbanization and transportation. Electric vehicles, shared mobility, and smart transportation systems are some of the promising approaches that can transform our mobility landscape. However, to achieve widespread adoption, collaboration between governments, private sector players, and individuals is crucial. Only through collective efforts can we build a sustainable and resilient transportation future for all.

Chapter 3: Sustainable Mobility Solutions

Active transportation, specifically walking and cycling, has gained significant attention in recent years as environmentally conscious modes of transportation. The benefits of these modes extend beyond individual health to issues of environmental sustainability and building livable communities. This movement towards active transportation has been fueled by a collective effort to reduce greenhouse gas (GHG) emissions, combat climate change, and create more accessible urban environments.

Walking and cycling offer a number of environmental advantages over other forms of transportation. First and foremost, these modes are carbon-neutral since they do not require the use of fossil fuels. This is in stark contrast to vehicles such as cars and motorcycles, which are responsible for a large portion of GHG emissions globally. By opting for walking or cycling over motorized transportation, individuals contribute to lowering air pollution and combatting climate change.

Additionally, active transportation reduces the need for road constructions and widening. Cities investing in walking and cycling infrastructure can decrease their dependency on automobiles, reducing the strain on land and resources that would be otherwise used to construct and maintain roads. By prioritizing walking and cycling, cities signify commitments to smart and sustainable urban design that promote efficient land use and enhance the quality of life for residents.

Furthermore, active transportation promotes the concept of complete streets, where roads are thoughtfully designed to accommodate all users including pedestrians and cyclists. This entails dedicating space for safe sidewalks and bike lanes, as well as traffic calming measures to ensure the safety of vulnerable road users. By implementing complete streets policies, cities can encourage more individuals to walk or cycle, making urban environments more people-oriented and inclusive.

Studies consistently show a positive correlation between active transportation and real estate value. Walkable neighborhoods are highly sought after, as they offer convenience, amenities, and a healthier lifestyle. The demand for housing in areas with good walking and cycling infrastructure increases property values, leading to economic benefits for the community. Increased investments in these modes also have the potential to boost local economies, as money once spent on gas or vehicle maintenance is redirected towards local businesses and services.

Additionally, active transportation brings social benefits by fostering increased social interactions. Walking and cycling promote face-to-face interactions and create opportunities for people to engage and connect with their surroundings and each other. This can contribute to stronger community cohesion, improved mental health, and decreased social isolation. Moreover, walking and cycling are accessible to people of all ages and abilities, making them inclusive and equitable modes of transportation.

To further promote walking and cycling as environmentally conscious modes, it is crucial to overcome existing barriers. These include limited infrastructure, safety concerns, and the perception of active transportation being inconvenient or time-consuming. Governments, policymakers, and urban planners need to invest in safe and accessible infrastructure, implement integrated policies, and promote active transportation through education and awareness campaigns. In addition, creating incentives such as subsidies and tax breaks can encourage individuals to opt for active transportation.

In conclusion, walking and cycling offer immense potential to reduce GHG emissions, combat climate change, and create livable communities. Beyond individual health benefits, these modes contribute to sustainable development, efficient land use, and a sense of community. By prioritizing walking and cycling, cities can pave the way towards a greener, healthier, and more equitable future.

3.1 Active Transportation: Walking and Cycling as Environmentally Conscious Modes

Carpooling and ride-sharing are methods of transportation that involve people sharing rides in order to minimize the number of vehicles on the road. This collaborative approach to travel has gained popularity in recent years due to its potential for reducing emissions and alleviating traffic congestion. By sharing a ride, multiple people can travel to a common destination together, reducing the need for individual vehicles and therefore decreasing carbon emissions and other pollutants released into the atmosphere.

Collaborative travel offers numerous benefits for both individuals and the environment. Firstly, by sharing a car, passengers are able to split the cost of fuel and tolls, resulting in substantial cost savings. Additionally, carpooling and ride-sharing can reduce travel time, as fewer vehicles on the road means less congestion and traffic jams. By avoiding the stress of daily traffic, passengers can experience a more relaxed and enjoyable journey. Furthermore, carpooling and ride-sharing can foster social connections, as passengers have the opportunity to interact and build relationships with one another, making the commute a more enjoyable experience overall.

From an environmental standpoint, carpooling and ride-sharing have a significant impact on reducing emissions. By utilizing one vehicle to transport multiple passengers, the amount of greenhouse gases emitted per person is significantly reduced. This directly contributes to the fight against climate change and helps improve air quality, particularly in heavily congested cities. Moreover, reduced traffic congestion resulting from carpooling and ride-sharing can lead to smoother traffic flow, minimizing the start-stop driving that contributes to excessive fuel consumption and emissions. This improved traffic flow is beneficial not only for the environment but also for the mental and physical well-being of commuters.

To facilitate carpooling and ride-sharing, several technological platforms have emerged, offering convenient and efficient ways to connect riders and drivers. These platforms, often in the form of mobile applications, allow users to input their starting point and destination, find potential ride-sharing partners, and coordinate their trips accordingly. This digital accessibility has revolutionized the carpooling industry, making it easier and more feasible for individuals to opt for collaborative travel rather than driving alone.

While carpooling and ride-sharing offer promising solutions to reducing emissions, adoption rates remain relatively low in many parts of the world. One significant barrier is the perception of inconvenience and a lack of flexibility that may arise from sharing a ride with others. Some individuals prefer the comfort and freedom of traveling alone and may perceive carpooling as cumbersome and restrictive. Additionally, there may be logistical challenges in coordinating schedules and routes, particularly for those with irregular work hours or multiple destinations.

To overcome these barriers, governments and organizations can play a vital role in promoting and incentivizing carpooling and ride-sharing initiatives. This can be done through the implementation of designated carpool lanes, reduced toll fees for shared vehicles, tax incentives for carpoolers, and public awareness campaigns highlighting the benefits of collaborative travel. By addressing these concerns and providing tangible incentives, carpooling and ride-sharing can become more widely adopted, resulting in a significant reduction in emissions and a greener, more sustainable transportation system.

Carpooling and ride-sharing have the potential to make a substantial impact in mitigating climate change and reducing emissions. By encouraging and incentivizing collaborative travel, individuals and governments can actively contribute to sustainable transportation practices while experiencing the many benefits that come with shared journeys. The shift toward a greener and more efficient transportation system is essential for the future of our planet, and carpooling and ride-sharing are promising strategies to help us pave the way towards a more sustainable future.

3.2 Carpooling and Ride-sharing: Reducing Emissions through Collaborative Travel

The field of green technologies has seen significant advancements in recent years as the world continues to shift towards more sustainable and environmentally-friendly alternatives. Two prominent advancements in this field are the development of hydrogen fuel cells and biofuels, both of which offer promising solutions to reducing greenhouse gas emissions and dependence on fossil fuels.

Hydrogen fuel cells utilize the chemical reaction between hydrogen and oxygen to generate electricity, producing only water vapor and heat as byproducts. This makes hydrogen fuel cells a highly attractive option for transportation and power generation. The use of hydrogen as a fuel source is not only clean but also abundant, as it can be produced through various methods, such as water electrolysis or by extracting hydrogen from natural gas. Furthermore, hydrogen fuel cells have the advantage of being highly efficient, with conversion efficiencies as high as 60% or even greater.

Biofuels, on the other hand, are fuels derived from organic matter, such as plants and plant oils. Unlike fossil fuels, which are formed over millions of years through the decomposition of organic matter, biofuels can be produced within a relatively short period of time and are considered carbon-neutral. This means that the carbon released during the combustion of biofuels is offset by the carbon absorbed by the plants during their growth. In addition, biofuels can be blended with conventional fuels, such as gasoline and diesel, or used as standalone alternatives in transportation, providing a more sustainable option.

Both hydrogen fuel cells and biofuels offer several advantages over traditional fossil fuel-based technologies. They have the potential to significantly reduce greenhouse gas emissions, as they produce little to no pollutants during operation. This is especially crucial in sectors such as transportation, which accounts for a significant portion of global emissions. By transitioning to hydrogen fuel cells and biofuels, countries can effectively address climate change and work towards a greener future.

Additionally, the advancement of these technologies has also sparked innovations in infrastructure development. In order to fully embrace hydrogen fuel cells, for example, refueling stations must be established to make hydrogen readily available to consumers. Governments and private industries have been investing heavily in the construction of hydrogen refueling stations, especially in regions where the adoption of hydrogen-powered vehicles is more prevalent.

Similarly, the production and distribution of biofuels require the development of specialized processing plants and logistics chains. This has created economic opportunities in regions that are suited for biofuel production, such as areas with abundant biomass resources. The growth of these emerging industries not only promotes sustainable practices but also boosts local economies and generates employment opportunities.

Despite their potential and benefits, there are still challenges that need to be addressed in the widespread adoption of hydrogen fuel cells and biofuels. One major hurdle is the cost associated with these technologies. Currently, hydrogen fuel cells are expensive to produce and deploy, primarily due to the cost of platinum, a precious metal used as a catalyst in fuel cell electrodes. Similarly, the large-scale production of biofuels requires significant investments in feedstock cultivation, processing, and refining.

Another challenge lies in the development of appropriate regulations and policies to support the growth of these industries. Governments must provide necessary incentives, such as tax credits or subsidies, to promote the adoption of hydrogen fuel cells and biofuels. Moreover, standards for safety, storage, and distribution need to be established to ensure the efficient and safe integration of these technologies into existing infrastructures.

In conclusion, the advances in hydrogen fuel cells and biofuels offer promising solutions to the environmental challenges we face today. With their ability to reduce greenhouse gas emissions and provide more sustainable alternatives to fossil fuels, hydrogen fuel cells and biofuels have the potential to revolutionize multiple sectors, including transportation, power generation, and industrial processes. While there are obstacles to overcome, the ongoing investments and research in these green technologies are paving the way for a cleaner and more sustainable future.

3.3 Advances in Green Technologies: Hydrogen Fuel Cells and Biofuels

Urban planning plays a significant role in shaping sustainable transportation systems and promoting the development of mixed-use communities. These communities offer a diverse range of land uses within a compact area, allowing residents to have easy access to various amenities, services, and opportunities. By integrating different land uses, such as residential, commercial, and recreational areas, into one neighborhood, mixed-use communities can reduce the need for long-distance travel, encourage active transportation modes, and ultimately create a more sustainable and livable environment.

One of the key benefits of mixed-use communities is the reduction in commuting distances. Traditional city planning often separates residential areas from commercial or employment centers, forcing people to travel long distances to access their workplaces or other services. This reliance on private vehicles leads to traffic congestion, increased greenhouse gas emissions, and a higher dependency on fossil fuels. In contrast, mixed-use communities allow residents to work, shop, and play within a short distance from their homes, reducing the need for lengthy commutes. This not only saves time and money for individuals but also contributes to a more sustainable transportation system by decreasing the number of vehicle miles traveled.

Moreover, mixed-use communities promote sustainable transportation modes, such as walking, cycling, and public transit. The compact layout and diverse land uses encourage residents to choose active transportation options for their daily needs. By creating walkable neighborhoods with well-connected sidewalks, pedestrian-friendly streets, and bicycle lanes, urban planners can actively promote and prioritize these modes of transportation, leading to increased physical activity, reduced air pollution, and improved overall health and well-being. Accessible and well-designed public transit systems within mixed-use communities further encourage residents to rely less on personal vehicles, promoting the use of shared mobility options and reducing overall traffic congestion.

In addition to transportation-related benefits, mixed-use communities offer a range of social, economic, and environmental advantages. The diversity of land uses creates vibrant neighborhoods, fostering social interactions, and enhancing quality of life. The proximity of employment opportunities to residential areas allows for a better work-life balance and reduces disparities in accessibility to jobs. Small local businesses thrive in mixed-use communities, serving as economic engines and creating employment opportunities within the community. These factors contribute to the creation of a sustainable and resilient neighborhood where people actively participate in the local economy and feel a sense of community.

From an environmental perspective, mixed-use communities minimize land consumption and encourage efficient land use. By consolidating different activities within a compact area, excess land for roads, parking lots, and other infrastructures can be reduced. This efficiency leads to fewer greenhouse gas emissions, lower energy consumption, and better resource management. Mixed-use communities also promote sustainable building design and construction practices, setting higher standards for energy efficiency, water conservation, and waste reduction. These environmentally conscious approaches further contribute to the overall sustainability of these communities.

To promote mixed-use communities and sustainable transportation, urban planning strategies must prioritize connectivity, accessibility, and a diverse mix of land uses. This includes designing transportation networks that prioritize pedestrians, cyclists, and public transit, alongside the traditional focus on private vehicles. It requires creating zoning regulations that encourage mixed-use developments and regulations that reduce parking requirements, allowing for more efficient land use. Investments in infrastructure, such as sidewalks, bus stops, bike lanes, and transit stations, are also necessary to support and facilitate sustainable transportation options within these communities.

In conclusion, promoting mixed-use communities through urban planning is essential for sustainable transportation. These communities offer numerous benefits, including reduced commuting distances, increased reliance on active transportation modes, enhanced social and economic interaction, and improved environmental stewardship. By prioritizing connectivity, accessibility, and land use efficiency, urban planners can contribute to the creation of vibrant, livable environments where people have a range of amenities and services within easy reach. Through integrated planning, policymakers can encourage the development of mixed-use communities that shape sustainable transportation systems and provide an enhanced quality of life for all residents.

3.4 Promoting Mixed-Use Communities: Urban Planning for Sustainable Transportation

Government initiatives to encourage eco-friendly mobility play a crucial role in tackling climate change and promoting sustainable development. Eco-friendly mobility refers to modes of transportation that have a reduced impact on the environment, such as electric vehicles, public transportation systems, and cycling infrastructure. In this article, we will explore three policy interventions that governments can implement to promote eco-friendly mobility.

1. Incentives for Electric Vehicles:

The adoption of electric vehicles (EVs) is an effective way to reduce greenhouse gas emissions from the transportation sector. Governments can encourage EV adoption through various incentives. One common measure is providing subsidies or grants to lower the upfront cost of purchasing an electric vehicle. These financial incentives alleviate the perception that EVs are too expensive for many consumers and make them a more affordable option. Additionally, governments can offer tax credits for EV purchases or exemptions from tolls, parking fees, and vehicle registration charges. These incentives not only boost consumer interest in EVs but also stimulate market demand, driving innovation and the growth of the electric vehicle industry.

2. Investment in Public Transportation:

Public transportation systems are vital for reducing the number of private cars on the roads, mitigating traffic congestion, and lowering emissions. Governments can promote the use of public transportation by investing in infrastructure development, expanding existing networks, and increasing the frequency and reliability of services. Investments should focus on developing integrated networks that seamlessly connect different modes of public transport, including buses, trams, trains, and metros. Governments can also provide financial support to public transport operators to improve the quality of services, such as upgrading fleets with low-emission vehicles and implementing smart technologies to enhance efficiency. Improve public transportation accessibility in rural areas and incentivize the use of public transportation modes through discounted fares or monthly passes. By enhancing the quality and accessibility of public transportation, governments can encourage individuals to opt for sustainable modes of travel.

3. Cycling Infrastructures and Policies:

Promoting cycling infrastructure and policies is another effective policy intervention to encourage eco-friendly mobility. Governments can allocate funds and invest in the development of dedicated bicycle paths, lanes, and increased bicycle parking facilities. Implementing policies that prioritize the safety of cyclists, such as lower speed limits and traffic calming measures, also contribute to creating a conducive environment for cycling.

Furthermore, governments can provide financial incentives to individuals for purchasing bicycles or electric bikes. Encouraging employers to offer incentives like cycle schemes or providing tax benefits for employees who commute to work by bike can also motivate individuals to opt for cycling. By creating a cyclist-friendly infrastructure and implementing effective policies, governments can contribute towards promoting eco-friendly mobility and a healthier population.

In conclusion, government initiatives play a critical role in encouraging eco-friendly mobility. Through incentives for electric vehicles, investing in public transportation, and promoting cycling infrastructures and policies, governments can successfully reduce greenhouse gas emissions, alleviate traffic congestion, and create healthier and more sustainable transportation systems. These policy interventions can improve air quality, enhance public health, and contribute to the overall well-being of society, ultimately ensuring a greener and more sustainable future.

3.5 Policy Interventions: Government Initiatives to Encourage Eco-friendly Mobility

Chapter 4: The Role of Urban Planning

• • • •

URBAN PLANNING PLAYS a crucial role in shaping the form, function, and livability of cities. This chapter explores the various aspects and significance of urban planning in contemporary society. From historical perspectives to present-day challenges, we delve into the intricacies and importance of this field.

Historical Evolution of Urban Planning:

To understand the current role of urban planning, we must consider its historical evolution. The birth of urban planning can be traced back to ancient civilizations, where city designs and organizing principles were established. From the iconic city grid plan in Mohenjo-Daro to the grandeur of ancient Roman and Greek cities, the principles of urban planning find their roots in ancient times.

However, the modern practice of urban planning gained prominence during the Industrial Revolution. Rapid urbanization and the challenges that accompanied it necessitated centralized planning to address issues like housing, transportation, and sanitation. Urban planners emerged as professionals responsible for designing sustainable and functional cities.

Elements of Urban Planning:

Urban planning encompasses a wide range of activities and elements. It involves land-use planning, transportation planning, environmental design, infrastructure development, and community participation. An effective urban plan integrates these concerns to create a well-balanced and cohesive city that meets the needs of its residents.

Land-use planning establishes the appropriate mix of residential, commercial, and industrial areas. Zoning regulations and comprehensive plans guide the development and layout of different land uses, ensuring compatibility and preventing conflicts.

Transportation planning addresses the movement of people and goods within a city. It includes the provision of public transit systems, road networks, bicycle lanes, and pedestrian-friendly infrastructure. A well-designed transportation plan improves accessibility, reduces congestion, and promotes sustainable modes of transportation.

Environmental design focuses on creating a green and healthy urban environment. This includes the preservation of natural resources, the creation of open spaces and parks, and sustainable building practices. Aesthetics and public art also play a role in shaping the identity and vibrancy of a city.

Infrastructure development encompasses the provision of essential public services like water supply, sanitation, electricity, and telecommunications. Effective urban planning ensures that these services are accessible to all residents, promoting social equity and inclusivity.

Importance of Urban Planning:

Urban planning plays a vital role in addressing the challenges faced by cities today. It fosters economic development by attracting investments and creating job opportunities. A well-planned city becomes a hub of innovation and cultural activity, attracting residents, businesses, and tourists alike.

Additionally, urban planning promotes sustainability and resilience. It helps mitigate and adapt to the impacts of climate change by incorporating green infrastructure and sustainable building practices. By reducing sprawl and promoting compact development, urban planning minimizes the carbon footprint of cities.

Social equity is another crucial aspect of urban planning. It ensures that all residents, regardless of their socio-economic backgrounds, have access to essential services, housing, and amenities. Moreover, participatory planning processes empower communities to have a say in the decision-making process, promoting inclusivity and enhancing social cohesion.

Current Challenges and Future Directions:

Urban planning faces numerous challenges in the current era of rapid urbanization, population growth, and globalization. Cities are grappling with issues of affordable housing, traffic congestion, inadequate public transit, pollution, and social inequality. Urban planners are tasked with finding innovative solutions to tackle these complex problems.

The future of urban planning lies in adopting a holistic and sustainable approach. Embracing smart technology and data-driven decision-making can help optimize urban systems and improve efficiency. Collaboration between government, communities, and private stakeholders is also crucial for effective implementation and long-term success of urban plans.

• • • •

AS CITIES CONTINUE to grow and transform, the role of urban planning becomes even more critical. Balancing economic development, social equity, environmental sustainability, and resilience, urban planners shape the cities of tomorrow. By integrating the diverse elements and addressing current challenges, a well-executed urban plan creates livable, inclusive, and vibrant cities for future generations.

Chapter 4: The Role of Urban Planning

One of the many challenges faced by cities today is finding sustainable transportation solutions that can address the growing issue of traffic congestion and environmental concerns. Creating smart cities that prioritize efficient and environmentally-friendly transportation systems is crucial to building a more sustainable future.

Designing for sustainable transportation systems requires careful consideration of various factors, such as infrastructure, technology, and urban planning. It involves the integration of smart technologies and innovative approaches to optimize mobility, reduce emissions, and improve overall quality of life.

A key aspect of designing smart transportation systems is the development of infrastructure that supports sustainable modes of travel. This includes well-designed and connected networks for walking, cycling, and public transportation. By prioritizing these modes of transportation, cities can reduce the dependence on private vehicles, leading to decreased congestion and improved air quality.

Investing in smart technologies is also essential for creating sustainable transportation systems. This includes the implementation of intelligent transportation systems (ITS) that use advanced data analytics and real-time information to efficiently manage traffic flow. By using sensors, cameras, and other smart devices, these systems can monitor and control traffic signals, detect accidents or congestion, and provide real-time travel information to commuters. This not only enhances traffic management but also enables individuals to make informed decisions about the most sustainable modes of travel.

Additionally, designing for sustainable transportation involves promoting the use of electric vehicles (EVs) and alternative fuels. Governments and city planners should invest in the installation of charging stations for EVs and incentivize their adoption. This will not only contribute to reduced greenhouse gas emissions but also lead to improved air quality and less noise pollution.

Urban planning plays a critical role in designing for sustainable transportation systems. Cities need to prioritize compact and mixed-use development, with a focus on creating walkable and bike-friendly neighborhoods. This means ensuring that essential services and facilities are within walking or cycling distance, reducing the need for long commutes and unnecessary car trips.

Furthermore, implementing smart transportation systems requires collaboration between various stakeholders, including government agencies, urban planners, technology companies, and citizens. By involving the community in the decision-making process and gathering feedback, cities can better understand the needs and preferences of their residents, resulting in more effective and sustainable transportation solutions.

In conclusion, creating smart cities that prioritize sustainable transportation systems is imperative for addressing traffic congestion and environmental concerns. By considering factors such as infrastructure, technology, and urban planning, cities can design efficient and environmentally-friendly transportation systems. This includes the integration of smart technologies, the development of infrastructure to support sustainable modes of travel, and promoting the use of EVs and alternative fuels. Ultimately, creating smart cities that prioritize sustainable transportation will lead to improved mobility, reduced emissions, and enhanced quality of life for its residents.

4.1 Creating Smart Cities: Designing for Sustainable Transportation Systems

Integrating land-use and transportation is a critical element of efficient city development. It involves designing urban areas that facilitate sustainable and efficient transportation modes such as walking, cycling, and public transportation, while simultaneously minimizing the need for private vehicle use. This integration holds immense potential for creating healthier, more equitable, and more sustainable cities for people and the environment.

By effectively integrating land-use and transportation, cities can reduce congestion and minimize traffic-related emissions. This can be achieved by designing compact, mixed-use neighborhoods that provide people with easy access to work, schools, shopping, and recreational facilities. When these destinations are within a reasonable distance, people are more likely to walk, cycle, or use public transit, instead of relying on individual vehicles. These non-motorized modes of transportation not only reduce congestion but also have positive impacts on air quality and public health.

In addition to the environmental benefits, integrated land-use and transportation planning has the potential to improve social equity. Well-designed cities can ensure that all residents, including those from low-income communities, have convenient access to basic services and job opportunities. This can be achieved by locating affordable housing closer to public transportation hubs and employment centers. It also helps to reduce disparities in transportation options between different neighborhoods, which is often a barrier to upward social mobility for disadvantaged communities.

Integrating land-use and transportation can also contribute to economic vibrancy and vitality. Efficient transportation systems make it easier for individuals to access job opportunities, boosting labor market efficiency. Well-connected cities encourage investment and economic growth by supporting industries and commerce. Furthermore, integrated planning can result in cost savings for both individuals and governments. Reduced reliance on private vehicles means lower fuel and maintenance costs for individuals, while cities can save on road infrastructure investments if more people choose sustainable transportation options.

MOVING TOWARDS SUSTAINABILITY: A GREEN JOURNEY IN TRANSPORTATION

Implementing integrated land-use and transportation planning requires a holistic approach to urban development. It involves adopting policies that encourage higher-density development along transit corridors, promoting the mix of uses in neighborhoods, and prioritizing investments in non-motorized infrastructure like sidewalks, bike lanes, and pedestrian-friendly amenities. Local governments can collaborate with public transport operators to ensure seamless connections between different modes of transportation and provide incentives for developers to incorporate sustainable transportation elements in their projects.

However, achieving efficient city development through integrated land-use and transportation planning is not without challenges. It requires the involvement and coordination of multiple stakeholders, including city planners, transport authorities, developers, and community representatives. Overcoming resistance to change and altering ingrained transportation habits can be a significant hurdle. Additionally, the upfront costs of implementing infrastructure improvements and establishing alternative transportation options can pose financial challenges, particularly for cash-strapped municipalities.

Despite these challenges, the long-term benefits of integrated land-use and transportation planning far outweigh the short-term difficulties. By creating cities that prioritize sustainable transportation options and compact urban development, we can ensure a better quality of life for residents, promote environmental sustainability, enhance social equity, and foster economic prosperity. Through collaboration, innovation, and a commitment to long-term planning, cities can create a future where transportation and land-use work in harmony for the benefit of all.

4.2 Integrating Land-use and Transportation: Efficient City Development

Public spaces play a crucial role in promoting active transportation. They provide people with pleasant environments where walking and cycling are both safe and enjoyable. To create pedestrian-friendly infrastructure, city planners and architects must consider various factors such as walkability, safety, accessibility, and aesthetic appeal.

One of the key elements of a pedestrian-friendly infrastructure is walkability. A walkable city is one that has well-connected and well-designed pedestrian pathways. Sidewalks should be wide enough to accommodate both pedestrians and cyclists comfortably. They should also be smooth and free of obstacles, ensuring a seamless and pleasant walking experience.

Furthermore, walkability can be enhanced by creating zones free of vehicular traffic. These car-free zones, commonly referred to as pedestrian malls or pedestrian streets, prioritize pedestrians over vehicles. They create an inviting environment for people to walk, linger, and engage in various activities. These car-free zones can be implemented in city centers, commercial areas, and popular tourist destinations.

Safety is another crucial aspect of pedestrian-friendly infrastructure. A well-designed public space ensures the safety of pedestrians by implementing various measures. Proper street lighting, marked crosswalks, and traffic calming mechanisms can significantly enhance pedestrian safety. Installations such as speed humps, pedestrian islands, and curb extensions can reduce vehicle speeds and make crossings safer.

Accessible infrastructure is vital to encourage active transportation for all members of the community. Public spaces must comply with accessibility regulations, ensuring they are usable by individuals with disabilities. This involves providing wheelchair ramps, tactile paving, and audible pedestrian signals. An inclusive environment benefits not only those with disabilities but also families with strollers and seniors who may require additional assistance.

Aesthetic appeal is also a significant factor in promoting active transportation. Beautifully designed public spaces have a positive impact on people's desire to walk or cycle. Incorporating greenery, public art, and seating areas can create inviting and attractive environments that encourage people to explore on foot. Enhancing the aesthetics of a public space also contributes to a sense of community pride and can increase the overall livability of an area.

In addition to these physical elements, encouraging active transportation requires partnerships between various stakeholders. Collaboration between city planners, transportation departments, and community organizations can help in creating comprehensive plans that prioritize pedestrians and cyclists. Engaging with local residents to understand their needs and preferences is also a crucial step to design public spaces that truly benefit the community.

Public spaces and pedestrian-friendly infrastructure go hand-in-hand in promoting active transportation. By considering factors such as walkability, safety, accessibility, and aesthetics, cities can create environments that encourage people to embrace walking and cycling. Making these changes will not only improve the health and well-being of individuals but also contribute to a more sustainable and vibrant community.

4.3 Public Spaces and Pedestrian-friendly Infrastructure: Encouraging Active Transportation

Transit-oriented development (TOD) and walkability strategies play a crucial role in prioritizing public transportation. These strategies aim to create communities that are accessible, convenient, and sustainable for residents. By integrating land use, transportation, and infrastructure planning, TOD and walkability strategies promote the use of public transportation, encourage walking and biking, and reduce car dependence.

One key aspect of TOD is the creation of transit hubs or nodes, which are areas centered around transit stations. These nodes facilitate easy access to various modes of public transportation, including trains, buses, and light rail systems. By locating high-density housing, retail, and public amenities near transit stations, TOD creates a seamless connection between residential areas and transportation options. This encourages residents to rely on public transportation for their daily commute, reducing traffic congestion and promoting a more sustainable travel option.

Furthermore, TOD focuses on creating mixed-use developments, where residential, commercial, and recreational activities are clustered together. This approach fosters a vibrant atmosphere where residents can live, work, and play within walking distance of their homes. By reducing the need for long car trips, TOD promotes walkability and minimizes carbon emissions. It also leads to increased social interaction and community engagement, as people are more likely to walk and engage with their surroundings when amenities are close by.

In addition to TOD, walkability strategies play a crucial role in prioritizing public transportation. Walkability refers to the ease and safety of walking within a community, including features like sidewalks, crosswalks, and pedestrian-friendly designs. When communities prioritize walkability, they create an environment that is conducive to pedestrian travel. This has significant benefits for public transportation, as it encourages people to walk to and from transit stations or bus stops. By reducing dependence on personal vehicles, walkability strategies contribute to a more sustainable transportation system and help alleviate traffic congestion.

To prioritize walkability, communities need to invest in pedestrian infrastructure. This includes designing and maintaining sidewalks, installing pedestrian crossings and signals, and ensuring adequate lighting and safety measures. Additionally, mixed-use and higher-density developments contribute to walkability by placing amenities and services within easy walking distance for residents.

Implementing TOD and walkability strategies requires collaboration among different stakeholders, such as urban planners, transportation agencies, developers, and community organizations. Effective transit-oriented development involves coordinating land use planning with transportation infrastructure investments to ensure that they support each other. Similarly, enhancing walkability requires close cooperation between transportation and urban design professionals to ensure safe and accessible pedestrian infrastructure.

In conclusion, prioritizing public transportation requires the implementation of transit-oriented development and walkability strategies. These approaches create communities that are accessible, convenient, and sustainable, reducing dependence on personal vehicles and promoting the use of public transportation. By integrating land use and transportation planning, investing in transit hubs and pedestrian infrastructure, and fostering mixed-use and walkable neighborhoods, cities can create a more efficient and sustainable transportation system for their residents.

4.4 Prioritizing Public Transportation: Transit-oriented Development and Walkability Strategies

Strengthening non-motorized transportation networks is crucial in promoting active and sustainable modes of transportation. Safe and connected cycling and walking paths play a vital role in encouraging people to choose to walk or cycle instead of relying solely on motorized vehicles. In this article, we will delve into the importance of safe and connected cycling and walking paths and discuss how they can be strengthened.

One of the key benefits of safe and connected cycling and walking paths is that they increase safety for pedestrians and cyclists. With dedicated paths that are separate from roads, pedestrians and cyclists can feel more secure knowing that they are protected from heavy traffic. This is extremely important for vulnerable road users, such as children and older adults, who may not be as agile or capable of reacting quickly to dangers on the road. Creating spaces where pedestrians and cyclists have the right of way helps reduce the risk of accidents and promotes confidence in active transportation.

Additionally, safe and connected cycling and walking paths have a positive impact on public health. Encouraging walking and cycling as means of transportation helps reduce sedentary lifestyles, which are associated with various health problems like obesity and cardiovascular diseases. Providing accessible and well-maintained paths that connect different areas of a city or community promotes active lifestyles and encourages people to opt for these modes of transportation. The physical activity gained from walking and cycling also contributes to improved mental well-being and can help combat stress and anxiety.

Furthermore, safe and connected cycling and walking paths can benefit the environment by reducing carbon emissions. By encouraging people to shift from motorized vehicles to non-motorized transportation options, cities can significantly decrease their carbon footprint. This plays a crucial role in combating climate change and air pollution. Creating a network of paths that seamlessly connects different areas also increases the feasibility of using walking and cycling as a primary mode of transportation, as it eliminates barriers like having to navigate through busy streets or unsafe areas.

MOVING TOWARDS SUSTAINABILITY: A GREEN JOURNEY IN TRANSPORTATION

To strengthen non-motorized transportation networks and promote safe and connected cycling and walking paths, several strategies can be employed. First, urban planning should prioritize the development and maintenance of dedicated paths for pedestrians and cyclists. These paths should be integrated into the overall transportation infrastructure and designed with safety and accessibility in mind. This includes proper signage, well-designed intersections, and adequate lighting for nighttime use.

Additionally, community input and involvement are crucial in creating strong non-motorized transportation networks. Engaging with residents and conducting surveys or public consultations can help identify areas that require improved infrastructure and address specific needs or concerns. This collaborative approach ensures that the paths are designed to meet the requirements of the community and encourages active participation in using and maintaining these facilities.

Furthermore, it is essential to prioritize education and awareness campaigns to promote the use of safe and connected cycling and walking paths. Providing information on the benefits of active transportation and teaching road safety rules to cyclists and pedestrians can encourage more people to choose these modes of transportation. Additionally, initiatives like bike-sharing programs or workshops on cycling skills can enhance the knowledge and confidence of potential users.

In conclusion, strengthening non-motorized transportation networks through the development of safe and connected cycling and walking paths is crucial for promoting active and sustainable modes of transportation. These paths increase safety, improve public health, and help protect the environment. By prioritizing urban planning, engaging with the community, and promoting education and awareness, cities can create a network of paths that encourage people to choose walking and cycling as a viable means of transportation.

4.5 Strengthening Non-motorized Transportation Networks: Safe and Connected Cycling and Walking Paths

Chapter 5: Global Trends in Eco-friendly Transportation

• • • •

IN RECENT YEARS, THERE has been a growing concern about the environmental impact of transportation systems around the world. The transportation sector is a significant contributor to greenhouse gas emissions, air pollution, and noise pollution. In response to these concerns, global trends have emerged, leading to the development and adoption of eco-friendly transportation options. This chapter explores these trends, examining the push for sustainability, innovation, and policy changes shaping the future of transportation.

1. Green Vehicles:

One of the most noticeable trends in eco-friendly transportation is the emergence of green vehicles. Car manufacturers have been increasingly investing in research and development to create electric and hybrid vehicles. These vehicles rely on alternative fuels, such as electricity or a combination of electricity and gasoline, to power their engines. The advantages of these vehicles include reduced emissions and increased fuel efficiency, making them more environmentally friendly than traditional gasoline-powered vehicles. Furthermore, advancements in battery technology have resulted in increased driving ranges and faster charging times, making electric vehicles a viable option for long-distance travel.

2. Public Transportation Revitalization:

Efforts to reduce individual car usage have also led to a revitalization of public transportation systems. Many cities have expanded their public transportation networks, investing in new buses, trams, and trains. These vehicles are often fuel-efficient and emit fewer pollutants compared to private cars. Governments have introduced policies to incentivize public transportation use, such as reducing fares, implementing dedicated bus lanes, and improving infrastructure. These measures not only reduce traffic congestion but also provide affordable and sustainable transportation options for the general public.

3. Cycling and Walking Infrastructure:

Cities around the world are witnessing a surge in the construction of dedicated cycling and walking infrastructure. From bike lanes to pedestrian-friendly sidewalks, these initiatives aim to promote active modes of transport and reduce reliance on fossil fuel-powered vehicles. The introduction of shared bicycle systems and electric scooters has further increased the appeal of cycling as a viable transportation option. In addition to reducing emissions, cycling and walking promote better public health by encouraging exercise and reducing sedentary behaviors.

4. Intelligent Transportation Systems:

Technological advancements have also driven eco-friendly transportation trends through the implementation of Intelligent Transportation Systems (ITS). ITS integrates various technologies, including sensors, communication devices, and data analytics, to optimize traffic flows, reduce congestion, and improve fuel efficiency. Traffic signal synchronization, real-time traveler information, and dynamic route guidance are some examples of technologies employed to mitigate transportation-related environmental issues. By increasing the efficiency of existing road infrastructure, ITS helps minimize fuel consumption and emissions, resulting in a greener transportation system.

5. Adoption of Alternative Fuels:

Though electric vehicles have gained popularity, the search for alternative fuels in transportation has not ceased. Liquid petroleum gas (LPG), compressed natural gas (CNG), and biofuels have emerged as viable alternatives to gasoline and diesel. LPG and CNG, produced from readily available sources, emit fewer greenhouse gases and air pollutants. Biofuels, made from renewable sources such as vegetable oils and algae, offer carbon-neutral alternatives to conventional fuels. The adoption of these alternative fuels in public transportation, freight shipping, and even airplanes demonstrates a commitment to reducing the carbon footprint of the transportation sector.

. . . .

ECO-FRIENDLY TRANSPORTATION trends are not just limited to a few geographic regions; they transcend borders and reflect a global consciousness towards sustainable mobility. Governments, industries, and individuals have embraced these trends to address pressing environmental concerns. The continuation of investment in green vehicles, public transportation, cycling infrastructure, intelligent transportation systems, and alternative fuels will pave the way for a healthier and greener future. By embracing these trends, we can forge a path towards a more sustainable and eco-friendly transportation system that benefits both current and future generations.

Chapter 5: Global Trends in Eco-friendly Transportation

In recent years, there has been a growing concern about the environmental impact of transportation and a need for eco-friendly alternatives. Various countries around the world have taken initiatives to promote sustainable transportation, aiming to reduce carbon emissions and preserve the environment. This comparative analysis will explore eco-friendly transportation initiatives in five countries- Sweden, the Netherlands, Japan, China, and the United States, highlighting their key strategies and achievements.

Sweden:

Sweden, known for its commitment to sustainability, has implemented several eco-friendly transportation initiatives. One of its remarkable achievements is the promotion of electric vehicles (EVs) through incentives, such as tax exemptions, reduced parking fees, and toll-free roads for EV owners. Additionally, Sweden has an extensive network of charging stations, enabling EV owners to conveniently charge their vehicles across the country. These initiatives have led to a significant increase in the adoption of EVs in Sweden and a reduction in carbon emissions.

The Netherlands:

The Netherlands is a pioneer in sustainable transportation initiatives. Cycling is an integral part of the Dutch culture, and the country has invested heavily in cycling infrastructure. Well-maintained cycle lanes, bicycle highways, and secure parking facilities encourage people to choose cycling as a means of transport. Moreover, the Dutch government has provided financial incentives and tax advantages for purchasing electric bicycles, further promoting sustainable mobility.

Japan:

Japan, with its advanced technology and efficient transportation systems, has also made remarkable progress in eco-friendly initiatives. The country has introduced hydrogen fuel cell vehicles (FCVs) as a means of reducing dependence on fossil fuels. Various hydrogen refueling stations have been established throughout Japan, enabling FCV owners to refuel their vehicles conveniently. Moreover, Japan has also focused on developing efficient public transportation systems, including high-speed trains and electric buses, to reduce reliance on private automobiles.

China:

As the world's most populous country, China faces significant transportation challenges and environmental concerns. To tackle these issues, China has implemented several initiatives, including the development of an extensive high-speed rail network, investment in electric buses, and the promotion of bike-sharing programs. Chinese cities have witnessed tremendous growth in bike-sharing systems, wherein people can rent bicycles for short commutes. This has not only reduced the number of private vehicles on the road but also improved air quality in urban areas.

The United States:

While the United States may have been slower in adopting eco-friendly transportation initiatives, several cities and states have made notable efforts towards sustainability. Cities like San Francisco, Portland, and Seattle have invested in public transportation infrastructure, including electric buses and light rail systems. Some states also offer tax credits and financial incentives for purchasing electric vehicles. However, there is still significant room for improvement, as the country's vast size and dependence on private automobiles pose challenges for implementing comprehensive eco-friendly transportation systems.

· · · ·

COMPARATIVE ANALYSIS of eco-friendly transportation initiatives around the world reveals the diverse strategies implemented by countries to combat environmental challenges. Sweden's promotion of EVs, the Netherlands' emphasis on cycling infrastructure, Japan's focus on FCVs and efficient public transportation, China's bike-sharing programs, and the United States' initiatives in major cities showcase different approaches towards sustainability. By studying these initiatives and their resulting impact, countries can learn from each other's successes and failures, leading to more effective and inclusive eco-friendly transportation measures globally.

5.1 Comparative Analysis: Eco-friendly Transportation Initiatives around the World

In recent years, the focus on sustainability and environmental consciousness has gained significant momentum. This shift towards a more sustainable future is not limited to individuals or organizations; it extends to cities and even entire countries. This article sheds light on five success stories of cities and countries leading the charge towards sustainability, detailing their efforts and the impact they have made.

1. Copenhagen, Denmark:

Copenhagen is widely recognized as one of the greenest cities in the world and a pioneer in sustainable urban planning. The city has set ambitious targets to become carbon-neutral by 2025 and has made significant progress towards achieving them. Renowned for its extensive cycling infrastructure, which accounts for 62% of residents commuting to work or education, Copenhagen continues to implement measures to green its transportation system. Investments in public transportation, electric vehicles, and sustainable buildings have significantly reduced carbon emissions.

2. Bhutan:

Bhutan, a small South Asian country, uniquely measures its prosperity by Gross National Happiness rather than Gross Domestic Product. Recognizing the importance of environmental sustainability to overall happiness, Bhutan has committed to maintaining at least 60% forest cover and has surpassed this goal with over 70% coverage. Additionally, the country has placed a constitutional obligation on maintaining environmental sustainability, ensuring all development projects undergo strict environmental assessments. Bhutan's focus on hydropower generation ensures a majority of its energy comes from clean and renewable sources.

3. Costa Rica:

Costa Rica is a country that exemplifies sustainability through its actions and policies. The country has made impressive strides in renewable energy production and has set the ambitious goal of becoming carbon-neutral by 2050. Leveraging its abundant natural resources, Costa Rica generates electricity almost entirely from renewable sources, with 99% of its energy coming from renewable resources in 2020. Additionally, the country boasts a strong commitment to protecting biodiversity and has implemented initiatives that preserved over a quarter of its land as protected areas.

4. Curitiba, Brazil:

Curitiba, a city in southern Brazil, has positioned itself as a leading example of sustainable urban design. It is renowned for its innovative transportation system that combines bus rapid transit (BRT), designated bike paths, and pedestrian-friendly zones. Curitiba's integrated planning emphasizes social equity, efficient land use, and the preservation of green spaces. The city has successfully managed to provide efficient and affordable public transportation to its residents while reducing congestion and emissions.

5. New Zealand:

The island nation of New Zealand has taken substantial steps towards sustainability, particularly through legislation and policy. In 2019, the New Zealand government passed the Zero Carbon Act, committing the country to become carbon-neutral by 2050. The act requires the government to set emission reduction targets, establish carbon budgets, and create climate change adaptation plans. New Zealand boasts a unique ecosystem, and its commitment to sustainable agricultural practices, conservation efforts, and environmental protection make it a remarkable success story.

The examples of Copenhagen, Bhutan, Costa Rica, Curitiba, and New Zealand highlight the diverse approaches cities and countries can take to lead the way towards sustainability. These success stories demonstrate that ambitious goals and commitment to environmentally conscious policies can lead to significant strides in creating a more sustainable future. As more cities and countries follow their footsteps, we move closer to achieving global sustainability and ensuring a healthier planet for future generations.

5.2 Success Stories: Cities and Countries Leading the Charge towards Sustainability

In the ever-evolving world of business, one of the most critical challenges faced by organizations is the adaptation and implementation of best practices in different regions. While best practices serve as guidelines and benchmarks for excellence, they often need to be fine-tuned and tailored to suit the unique conditions and requirements of various geographical locations.

Adapting best practices can be a complex and multi-faceted task, as it involves addressing a range of challenges and opportunities. Listed below are some key considerations that organizations must take into account when adapting best practices in different regions:

1. Cultural Differences: Cultural factors significantly influence business practices, and what works in one location may not be as effective in another. Organizations need to be mindful of cultural nuances, communication styles, and socio-economic differences when adapting their practices. This often requires sensitivity, knowledge, and a willingness to invest time and resources in understanding and incorporating local customs and norms.

2. Legal and Regulatory Compliance: Different regions have their own specific legal requirements and regulations. Adapting best practices to meet these obligations ensures that organizations operate within the framework of local laws and fulfill their compliance responsibilities.

3. Language and Localization: Communication is key to successful implementation. Language barriers can hinder effective knowledge sharing and collaboration. Translating and localizing best practice documentation, codes of conduct, and other key resources are crucial steps towards ensuring clear understanding and adherence to the adapted practices.

4. Resource Allocation: Deploying best practices in different regions may require additional resources. Organizations need to assess the availability and allocation of resources required to support the implementation, whether it be training, personnel, or budgetary considerations. Proper resource planning is essential to ensure a seamless adaptation process.

5. Technology and Infrastructure: Technology is often a critical enabler of best practices. However, different regions may have varying levels of

technological infrastructure and connectivity. Organizations need to assess the digital readiness of a region and plan accordingly, taking into account the availability and suitability of technology infrastructure for effective implementation.

While challenges abound, there are also opportunities that arise from adapting best practices in different regions:

1. Knowledge Exchange and Innovation: Adapting best practices fosters knowledge exchange between different regions, allowing for insights and experiences to be shared. These valuable inputs can encourage innovation and lead to improved practices that transcend cultural boundaries.

2. Market Advantage: By effectively adapting and implementing best practices, organizations can increase their competitiveness in regional markets. The ability to seamlessly personalize and tailor practices to local needs can be a significant differentiator and a driver of market success.

3. Enhanced Reputation and Social Responsibility: Organizations that demonstrate a commitment to adapting best practices in different regions are often viewed as socially responsible and responsive to local needs. Such practices can enhance an organization's reputation, build trust with stakeholders, and contribute positively to the communities they operate in.

Adapting and implementing best practices in different regions requires careful planning, a comprehensive understanding of local contexts, and a willingness to be flexible and adaptable. Organizations that effectively navigate the challenges and opportunities associated with localization are well-positioned to thrive in today's global business landscape.

5.3 Challenges and Opportunities: Adapting Best Practices in Different Regions

International collaboration is crucial when it comes to tackling the challenges of climate change and building climate-resilient transportation systems. As climate change is a global issue, it requires global cooperation and efforts to effectively mitigate its impacts on transportation systems and ensure their resilience to future climate scenarios.

One of the most significant benefits of international collaboration is the sharing of knowledge, expertise, and experiences among countries. Different nations face different climate challenges, and by exchanging information and best practices, countries can develop a better understanding of how to adapt their transportation systems to climate change. This can include strategies for reducing greenhouse gas emissions from transport, improving infrastructure to withstand extreme weather events, and implementing sustainable transportation practices.

Furthermore, international collaboration allows countries to pool resources and coordinate efforts towards climate-resilient transportation systems. Climate change requires large-scale action, and no country can tackle it alone. By joining forces, countries can collectively invest in research, development, and innovation to improve transportation technology and infrastructure. This includes developing cleaner and more efficient vehicles, investing in low-carbon transportation modes like public transport and cycling, and creating better transportation networks and systems for resilience.

Several global initiatives and organizations are working towards collaborating internationally on climate-resilient transportation systems. For example, the United Nations Framework Convention on Climate Change (UNFCCC) aims to support countries in their efforts to combat climate change, including through transportation-related solutions. The Global Covenant of Mayors for Climate and Energy is another initiative that brings together cities from around the world to collaborate on reducing greenhouse gas emissions and building climate-resilient urban transport systems.

Many countries are also signing international agreements to foster collaboration and commitment to climate-resilient transportation. The Paris Agreement, for instance, obliges signatory countries to regularly report on their efforts to reduce greenhouse gas emissions, adapt to climate change, and promote sustainable development in their transportation sectors. These agreements create a platform for countries to share their progress, challenges, and solutions and learn from each other's experiences.

International collaboration is not only limited to governmental entities; it also involves academic institutions, non-governmental organizations, and private sector actors. Research institutions play a crucial role in developing new technologies, conducting studies, and providing evidence-based recommendations for climate-resilient transportation. Non-governmental organizations can help raise awareness, mobilize resources, and advocate for policy changes that support sustainable transportation. The private sector, including manufacturers, transport operators, and investors, can contribute technological advancements, funding, and expertise to develop climate-resilient transportation systems.

In conclusion, international collaboration is essential for building climate-resilient transportation systems. By sharing knowledge, pooling resources, and coordinating efforts, countries can develop effective strategies to adapt their transportation systems to climate change and mitigate their contribution to greenhouse gas emissions. Global initiatives, agreements, and organizations provide platforms for collaboration between governments, institutions, and private sector actors. By working together, countries can achieve a more sustainable and resilient transport sector that helps combat climate change and ensures the smooth functioning of transportation networks even in the face of future climate challenges.

5.4 International Collaboration: Global Efforts towards Climate-Resilient Transportation Systems

In conclusion, addressing climate change through eco-friendly transportation is crucial for our planet's future. As we continue to see the devastating effects of climate change, it is imperative that we take action now to reduce our carbon footprint.

The writing has provided extensive and meticulously detailed information on the various eco-friendly transportation options available to us. From electric vehicles to public transportation systems, there are several ways we can shift from traditional modes of transportation to greener alternatives.

This shift is not only beneficial for mitigating climate change but also for resolving other environmental issues such as air pollution and traffic congestion. By reducing our reliance on fossil fuels, we can significantly reduce harmful emissions and improve the air quality in our cities.

Moreover, transitioning to eco-friendly transportation solutions also has economic benefits. The writing has highlighted the potential for job creation in industries related to renewable energy and sustainable transportation. Not only will this help boost the economy, but it will also create a more sustainable future for future generations.

However, it is important to acknowledge that addressing climate change through eco-friendly transportation is not without challenges. The infrastructure required for widespread adoption of electric vehicles and efficient public transportation systems may require significant investments. Additionally, the shift will also demand changes in consumer behavior and preferences.

Despite these challenges, it is evident that taking steps towards a greener future through eco-friendly transportation is essential. The writing has provided a compelling case for why we should prioritize this issue and highlighted the numerous benefits it can bring.

By making informed decisions, supporting government policies that promote sustainable transportation, and adopting greener practices in our daily lives, we can collectively contribute towards a more sustainable and greener future. Every small step counts, and each individual action can make a significant difference when it comes to addressing climate change.

In conclusion, it is high time that we recognize our responsibility towards the environment and take action to mitigate the effects of climate change. Eco-friendly transportation is a tangible and effective way to reduce our carbon footprint and pave the way for a greener and more sustainable future. Let us come together and embrace these changes so that future generations can inherit a planet that is flourishing, healthy, and habitable.

Conclusion. Addressing Climate Change through Eco-friendly Transportation: Taking Steps towards a Greener Future

In conclusion, addressing climate change through eco-friendly transportation is crucial in taking steps towards a greener future. As evidenced by the rising global temperatures, melting ice caps, and increasing natural disasters, climate change is a significant threat that requires immediate action.

Transportation is a major contributor to greenhouse gas emissions, particularly through the burning of fossil fuels. However, embracing eco-friendly modes of transportation can significantly reduce these emissions and mitigate the effects of climate change. Electric vehicles, for example, produce zero emissions and have the potential to revolutionize the transportation sector. Their increasing popularity, advancements in technology, and the implementation of supportive policies are all indicators of a hopeful, greener future.

Furthermore, sustainable modes of public transportation, such as buses and trains, also play a vital role in addressing climate change. These systems can transport a large number of people, reducing the number of individual vehicles on the road. Encouraging greater usage of public transportation, investing in its infrastructure, and ensuring its affordability, accessibility, and efficiency are crucial steps towards creating a more sustainable transportation network.

In addition, active transportation, such as walking or cycling, promotes physical activity, reduces pollution, and decreases traffic congestion. Local governments can prioritize designing cities and neighborhoods with pedestrian and cyclist-friendly infrastructure, including safe sidewalks, bike lanes, and interconnected networks. By creating a conducive environment for active transportation, individuals can be incentivized to adopt healthier and more sustainable commuting options.

To effectively address climate change through eco-friendly transportation, collaboration between governments, industries, and individuals is crucial. Governments need to implement policies that support and incentivize the adoption of sustainable transportation alternatives. This could include tax incentives for electric vehicle purchases, regulations on emissions, and funding for the development of greener infrastructure.

Industries also have a significant role to play in reducing their transportation-related emissions. Companies can invest in electric vehicle fleets, incentivize sustainable commuting options for their employees, and promote telecommuting and videoconferencing to reduce the need for travel.

Lastly, individuals must acknowledge their responsibilities and actively engage in eco-friendly transportation practices. This could involve choosing public transportation over private cars whenever possible, carpooling or ridesharing, and using electric scooters or bikes for shorter trips. Additionally, individuals can advocate for greener transportation policies and spread awareness about the impact of transportation on climate change.

In conclusion, addressing climate change through eco-friendly transportation is an essential component of a greener future. By embracing electric vehicles, sustainable public transportation, and active transportation options, we can curb greenhouse gas emissions, improve air quality, and reduce our dependence on fossil fuels. Through collaboration between governments, industries, and individuals, we can collectively create a more sustainable and resilient future for our planet and future generations.

9 798822 370187